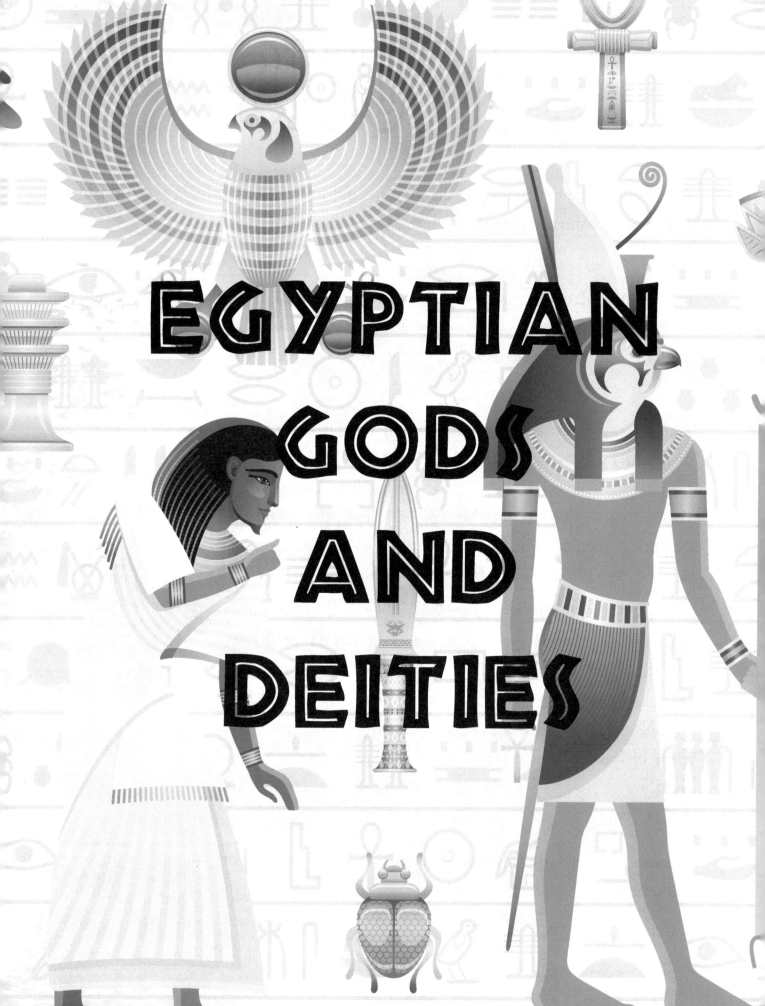

EGYPTIAN GODS AND DEITIES

ANUBIS

Anubis is the Egyptian God of the afterlife and mummification. He is the protector of lost souls. Anubis is one of the most ancient gods of Egypt.

He is represented as a black canid (a jackal most often), or a man with a jackal head. The black color is symbolic (jackals are not black). This color represents the decomposition of bodies as well as the fertile soil of the Nile Valley.

Anubis is the son of Osiris. According to the legend, Nephthys (Set's wife) was attracted by the beauty of Osiris (Set's brother). She then transformed herself to appear to him as Isis (Osiris' wife). Osiris, thinking he was with his wife Isis, slept with Nephthys. Nephthys then became pregnant and gave birth to Anubis. But she abandoned the child shortly after birth.

Isis discovered Nephthys' deception and learned of the child's existence. She found the abandoned child and adopted him. Set also learned of his wife's deception, and this explains in part his hatred for his brother Osiris. Anubis is regularly considered as Osiris' right hand man, and even his protector. He helps him to judge the souls of the dead.

Anubis is regularly invoked for his protection or for vengeance.

BASTET

Bastet is the goddess of the home, fertility and childbirth. She protects homes from evil spirits and diseases, especially for women and children. She also plays a role in the afterlife, as a guide for souls.

In the beginning, Bastet was represented as a lioness-headed woman, and was associated with the goddess Sekhmet. But this representation was aggressive, and she was later represented with more gentleness. Her most popular representation is that of a seated cat, looking ahead.

Bastet was a ruthless goddess for those who broke the laws and mistreated others.

Bastet is the daughter of the Sun God Ra, so she is associated with the concept of the Eye of Ra (the all-seeing eye).

Bastet was very popular in Ancient Egypt, especially from the second dynasty (2890 - 2670 BC).

HATHOR

Hathor is what is called a primitive goddess, from whom all other goddesses are derived. She is the goddess of joy and love. She is associated with women and health of body and mind. She was a very popular goddess.

Hathor is often represented as a woman with a cow's head, or a woman with just horns and a sun disk on her head. She can also be represented only by a cow.

She is considered to be the mother of the Sun God, Ra, and is often depicted alongside him in Egyptian art.

The name of Hathor means « domain of Horus » or « temple of Horus ». According to the legend, Horus (God of the sky) entered the mouth of Hathor every night to rest, and came out at dawn.

Hathor is linked to light, rejuvenation and rebirth.

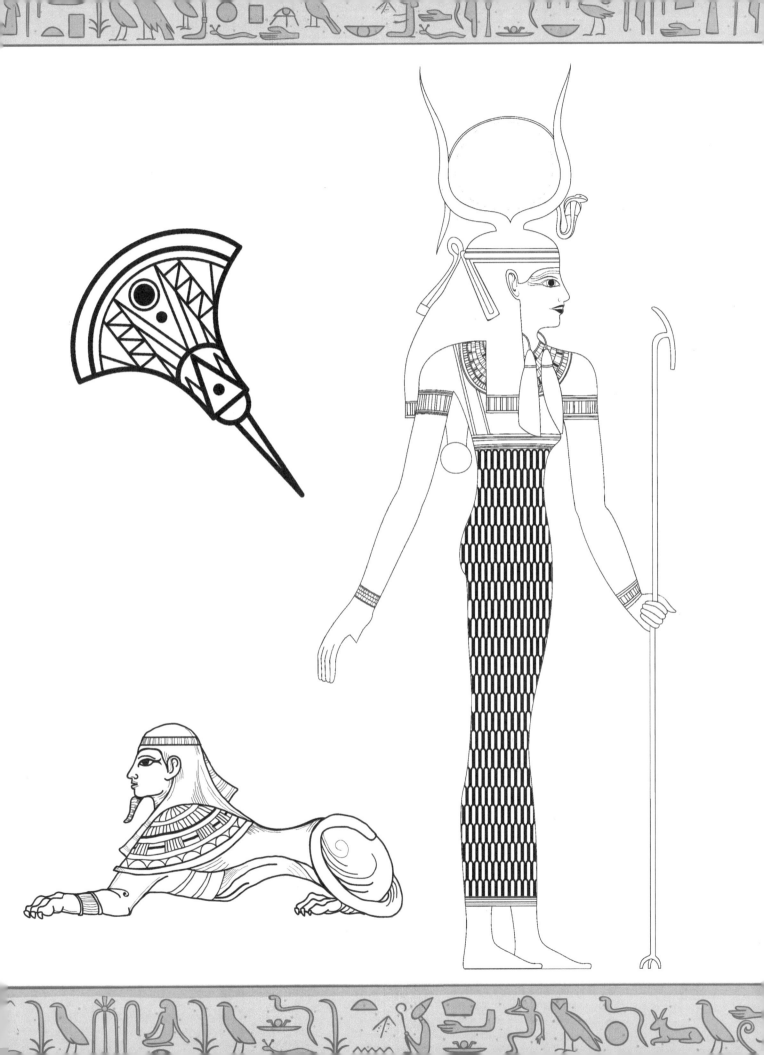

HORUS

Horus is the god of the sky, but he is actually associated with two distinct deities: Horus the Elder and Horus the Younger.

Horus the Elder, the last born of the five Original Gods, brother of Osiris, Isis, Set and Nephthys. In English he is called Horus the Great, and in Egyptian he is called Harwer or Haroeris. He is one of the most ancient gods, born from the union between Geb (the earth) and Nut (the sky), just after the creation of the world. He was in charge of protecting the sky and the sun.

Horus the Younger is the son of Osiris and Isis. He is sometimes called Horus the Child. He was a powerful god, associated with the sky and the sun, and also with the moon. He was a protector of the kingdom of Egypt, and the defender of order. After his battles with Set, Horus also became a god of war, often invoked before battles.

Horus is represented as a man with a hawk's head, sometimes with a double crown. He should not be confused with Ra, who is also a man with a hawk's head, but with a sun disk on his head.

ISIS

Isis is one of the most ancient goddesses and has become the most popular of all.

Her name comes from the word « eset », which means « seat » and refers to the throne of Egypt. She is considered the mother of every pharaoh.

Isis is represented as a woman, with a headdress representing a throne. This throne refers to the empty throne left by Osiris after his assassination. In some stories, she is also represented as a homeless woman, an old woman, or a widow.

Isis is described as a generous and very powerful protective goddess. In fact, she is also known as « Weret-Kekau », which means « great magic ».

Isis also had other names, depending on her role. According to legend, it was Isis who fertilized the soil by triggering the floods of the Nile. She was then called Sati. As the goddess who created life, she was called Ankhet.

With Osiris, her husband, Isis taught agriculture and medicine to the Egyptian people. It was also Isis who instituted marriage.

OSIRIS

Osiris is one of the most important gods of Ancient Egypt. He is the lord of the underworld and the judge of the dead. He is also the brother and husband of Isis.

Osiris is most often represented with a black or green skin, symbolizing the fertile mud of the Nile and the resurrection. Sometimes he is represented as a mummy.

Osiris is one of the first five gods, with Isis, Set, Horus and Nephthys. He was born from the union between Geb and Nut (Earth and Sky).

Osiris is very famous for a legend, the myth of Osiris.
Osiris is the first born. He ruled the earth with his wife Isis. He gave the Egyptian people laws, culture and education, agriculture and religion. During his reign, Egypt was a paradise where people were all equal and where famine did not exist.
Seth, his brother, was jealous of him. Moreover, he was very angry when he learned about the affair between Osiris and Nephthys (Set's wife).
Set had a coffin made. With cunning, he made Osiris enter it. He then closed the lid and threw it into the Nile. The coffin was carried away and disappeared.
Isis managed to find the coffin after months of searching, but Osiris was dead. She brought his body back to Egypt to give him back his life. But Set learned of this, and took Osiris' body again. He cut it into pieces and scattered it throughout the country.
Isis managed to find every part of the body, except for the penis, which had been eaten by a fish called the oxyrhynchus. This is why this fish was a forbidden food in ancient Egypt.
With the help of Nephthys, Thoth and Anubis, Isis mummified the body of Osiris. Osiris thus became the first mummy and the mythological basis of embalming. This process is to prevent and reverse the putrefaction of the bodies.

There are several versions of this legend. But Isis was able to give life to Osiris and then became pregnant with a son, Horus.

RA

Ra is the God of the Sun. He became one of the most important gods of Egypt, from the 25th century BC. Mainly associated with the sun, Ra nevertheless reigned over all parts of the world: Sky, earth, underworld.

Ra is represented in the form of a man with the head of a falcon, like Horus. But on his head, Ra has a solar disk and a snake wrapped around it. Horus wears the double crown.

Ra can also be represented as a ram, a scarab, a phoenix, or a bull.

According to legend, all life forms were created by Ra. Humans were created from his tears and sweat.

In one myth, humanity plotted against Ra. He then sent his eye in the form of the goddess Sekhmet to punish them.

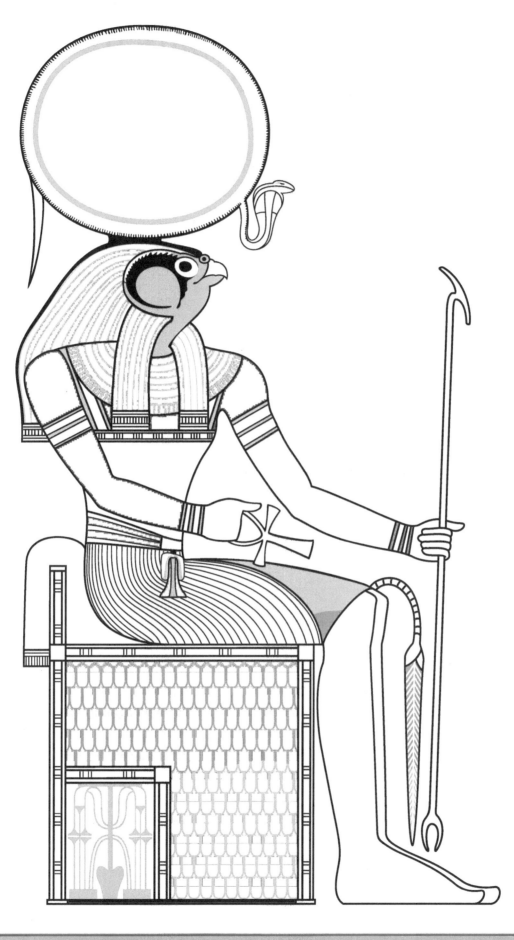

SEKHMET

Sekhmet is a warrior goddess, and a goddess of healing. She is considered as the protector of the pharaohs, even after their death.

She is represented as a woman with the head of a lioness, or simply as a lioness.

Sekhmet is often associated with the goddesses Bastet and Hathor.

Sekhmet is considered the daughter of Ra, and was the manifestation of his vengeance. She was said to spit fire and her breath formed deserts.

In myth, Ra sends Sekhmet to Earth to destroy the mortals who have conspired against him. Sekhmet's bloodlust was considerable. She destroyed almost all of humanity. To stop her, Ra poured beer dyed red to look like blood. Sekhmet drank so much that she became drunk. She stopped the massacre and fell asleep. When she woke up, she returned peacefully to Ra.

SET

Set, also known as Seth and Suetekh, was the god of war, chaos and storms. He is the brother of Osiris, Isis and Horus the elder. He is also the husband and brother of Nephthys.

His name is usually translated as « instigator of confusion » and « destroyer ».

He is often represented as a man with a dog's head, called Sha. Sometimes he is depicted as a red beast.

Set is known to be the first murderer in history by killing his brother Osiris. He also tried to murder Horus the Younger.

Set represents evil, but sometimes he does good: According to a legend, Set saved Ra from the serpent Apophis. Apophis was an evil creature who tried to stop the sun. He wanted to stop Ra's journey across the sky. Every night, Apophis hypnotized Ra. Set was able to resist the snake's deadly gaze, and repelled it with his spear. Thus Set ensured the rising of the sun.

Set was also considered a benefactor who helped people in life or in death.

SOBEK

Sobek, also called Sebek, was a god associated with crocodiles, the powers of the pharaoh, fertility and military acts. He was also invoked for protection from the dangers of the Nile.

Sobek was represented as a crocodile, or as a man with a crocodile head.

Sobek was above all an aggressive deity, like his animal protector, the great Nile crocodile.

However, in many myths, he shows benevolence. He would have even helped Isis to heal Osiris (in the myth of Osiris).

In Ancient Egypt, crocodiles were bred for religious reasons as the incarnation of Sobek. When they died, they were mummified. Many mummified crocodiles have been found, and some with mummified baby crocodiles in their mouths. The crocodile is one of the few reptiles to care for its offspring. These mummifications were probably intended to emphasize the protective aspects of Sobek, for he protected the people as crocodiles protect their young.

THOTH

Thoth is the Egyptian god of writing, magic, balance, wisdom and the moon. He is a very important god in Ancient Egypt. According to the legend, Thoth created himself.

Thoth is often represented as a man with the head of an ibis.

His name was often used by the pharaohs. For example the pharaoh Thutmose, which means « born of Thoth ».

Thoth presided over the judgment of the dead with Osiris in the Hall of Truth. Souls who feared they would not pass this judgment often sought Thoth's help.

Thoth was the husband of Seshat, the goddess of writing, guardian of books, and protector of librarians.

Finally, Thoth was the protector of scribes. According to the stories, before writing, the scribes poured a drop of ink in the honor of Thoth.

ABOUT DEITIES

There were many other Egyptian deities.

However, it is difficult to know exactly how many there were. Some legends have been intertwined for 3000 years.

It is considered that there were between 700 and 800 deities in total, but only about fifty were very present in the stories.

Some gods were represented with heads of ram, frog, snake, hippopotamus, bull. Others took the appearance of cobras, scorpions, and fish.

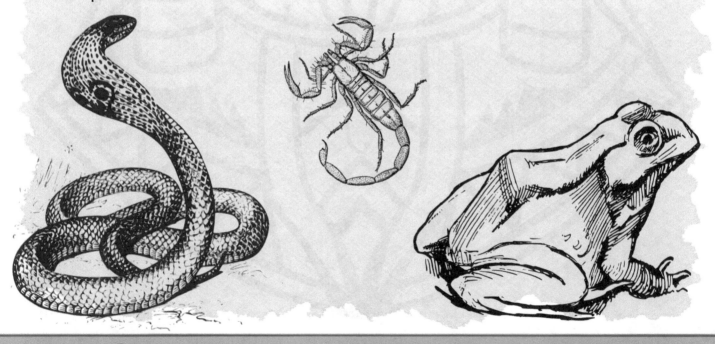

EGYPTIAN PHARAOHS AND QUEENS

AKHENATEN

Akhenaten was a pharaoh of the 18th dynasty. He was born in 1353 BC, and died in 1336 BC.

He is also known as Akhenaton, or Ikhnaten. His names all mean « success for the god Aten ».

At his birth, Akhenaten was called Amenhotep IV, son of Amenhotep III. Then he converted to the cult of the god Aten and took the name of Akhenaten. Aten was a unique god. Moreover, Akhenaten imposed this new cult on his people, sometimes in a rather brutal way. According to historians, this was the first monotheistic state religion in the world. At the death of the pharaoh, the cult of Aten fell into oblivion.

Akhenaten was the husband of Nefertiti, and father of Tutankhamun.

CLEOPATRA

Cleopatra is a very famous queen, but it is necessary to know that there were several queen Cleopatras. The one that everyone knows is in fact Cleopatra VII. She is the last queen of Egypt before its annexation by Rome.

Cleopatra was not Egyptian. She was Greek. She was indeed part of the Ptolemaic dynasty that ruled Egypt after the death of Alexander the Great (who founded Alexandria).

According to the stories, she spoke several languages, was charming and was a very efficient diplomat.

Cleopatra was a powerful queen, but she is best known for her love affairs: First with Julius Caesar, then with Mark Antony, a Roman general.

Moreover, Caesar defeated Cleopatra and Mark Antony at the battle of Actium in 31 BC. The reign of the queen then ended. Cleopatra committed suicide the following year, to avoid the humiliation of being exposed as a prisoner. According to the stories, she would have let a snake bite her, or would have drunk poison.

KHUFU / KHEOPS

Khufu, also known as Kheops, was a pharaoh of the 26th century BC.

He is known to be the pharaoh who built the Great Pyramid of Giza (also called the Pyramid of Khufu or Kheops), one of the 7 wonders of the ancient world.

It is not clear how long Khufu ruled Egypt. Historical documents contradict each other. According to some, he would have reigned 23 years, and for others more than 60 years.

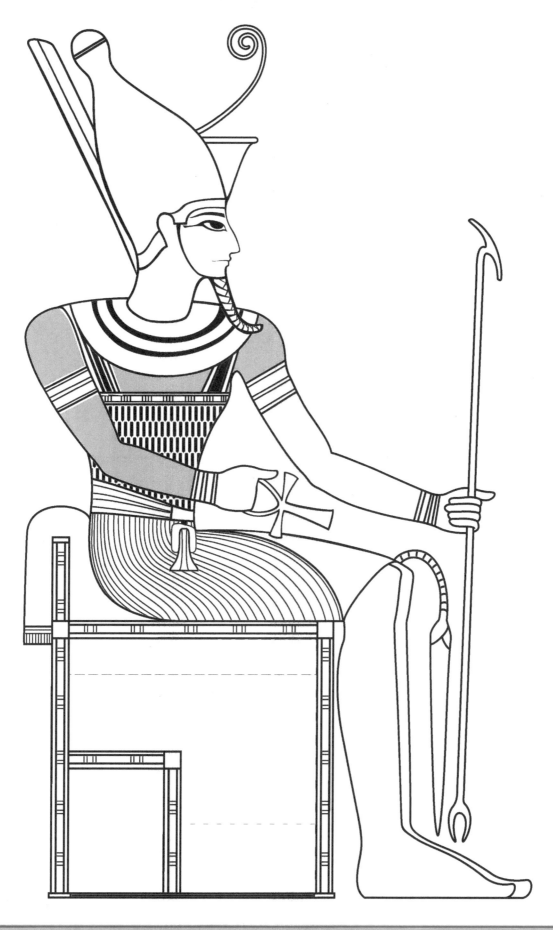

NEFERTITI

Nefertiti was the wife of the pharaoh Akhenaton. Her name means « the beautiful one came ». There is a very famous bust of this queen, made by the sculptor Thutmose (or Thoutmosis) and discovered in 1912.

Nefertiti is the most famous queen of Egypt. She would have been engaged to her future husband at the age of 11 years.

The couple had 6 daughters, but no son. On his side, Akhenaten had 2 sons with another wife (named Kiya), among them Tutankhamun.

According to the stories, the royal couple was deeply devoted to each other, and constantly together.

Nefertiti reigned with Akhenaten until his death. After that, she disappeared from the historical records.

RAMSES II

Ramses II (or Ramesses II) lived from 1279 to 1213 BC.

He had a relatively long reign for the time. He was also called the builder king, because he built many monuments.

He apparently had a reputation as a great warrior, especially after the battle of Kadesh.

Ramses II is often considered as the pharaoh opposed to Moses in the book of Exodus, at least for those who consider that the events of this story have a historical basis. Yet there is no record of his name in the Torah.

Ramses II lived to the age of 96. He is said to have had more than 200 wives (wives and mistresses), almost 100 sons and at least 60 daughters.

His reign was so long that most Egyptians had only known him as pharaoh. When he died, the people believed that the end of the world was coming with the death of their king.

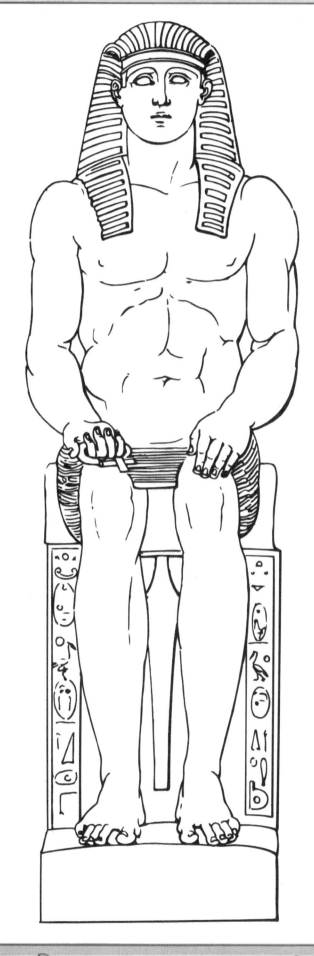

TUTANKHAMUN

Tutankhamun, also known as Tutankhamen and King Tut, was born in 1336 BC. He is the son of the pharaoh Akhenaton.

He died in 1327 BC, under mysterious conditions.

He is the most famous pharaoh. His name means "living image of the God Amun".

His golden sarcophagus became a symbol of Ancient Egypt. His tomb was discovered in 1922 by Howard Carter, a famous archaeologist. His tomb, located in the Valley of the Kings, was in perfect condition.

It was thought that Tutankhamun was a pharaoh of little importance, but the discovery of his tomb changed the opinion of historians. We know today that he put a lot of order in the chaos left by the political, economic and religious reforms of his father.

He probably would have done much more if he had not died so young.

Some say he died in a chariot accident. Others say he died of bone disease or malaria. It would also seem, according to recent studies, that Tutankhamun was born from an incest between Akhenaten and his sister. Marriage between brother and sister was common at that time.

ABOUT PHARAOS

Historians divide up the timeline of Ancient Egyptian history by the dynasties of the Pharaohs. A dynasty was when one family maintained power, handing down the throne to an heir. There are considered to be 31 dynasties over the 3000 years of Ancient Egyptian history.

It is more likely that there were about 200 pharaohs and 6 queens.

The first pharaoh is called Menes. Around 3100 BC, he united the north and the south of Egypt into one kingdom.

The last ruler of Egypt was a woman: Cleopatra.

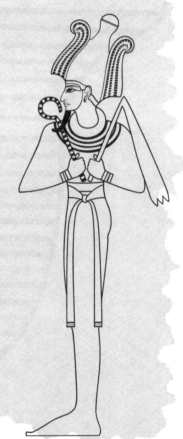

The youngest pharaoh is probably Pepy II became Pharaoh at the age of 6. He would rule Egypt for 94 years.

LIFE
IN ANCIENT
EGYPT

EGYPTIANS

At the time of the pharaohs, nine out of ten Egyptians were farmers. They did not own their land, which belonged to the pharaoh. There were also craftsmen, and then more noble but rare professions, like scribe for example.

For the farmers, life was quite hard. Their life was organized around the floods of the Nile (which fertilized the soil in particular).

The Egyptians had developed irrigation to water the crops, they had built dykes and basins to retain the water.

In times of flooding, it was impossible to cultivate the land. Often, farmers and craftsmen worked on construction sites (pyramids, monuments).

At the end of the floods, the farmers took advantage of the still soft soil to plow and sow.

Bread and beer were the main foodstuffs of the Egyptians. The farmers cultivated the cereals (barley and wheat) necessary for their production.

After the harvest, the grain was stored in large granaries, silos.

It should be noted that the people were generally very poor. The pharaoh and the priests took most of the crops and agricultural products. This is how the people paid the taxes.

THE NILE

The Nile is the longest river in Africa. It has been considered the longest river in the world, but recent studies show that the Amazon River is slightly longer.

The Nile is 6650 kilometers long, but some scientists estimate its length at 6800 kilometers.

The Nile comes from two distinct sources: The White Nile, which originates in Equatorial Africa, and the Blue Nile, which originates in the Abyssinian plateaus.

In ancient Egypt, the Nile was considered the source of all life. There are many myths concerning the Nile, or referring to it.

The Nile Delta is probably the most important area, both geographically and historically. About 150 kilometers from the Mediterranean coast, at the level of Cairo, the Nile separates into several branches. It forms a marshy area, with a very rich fauna and flora.

Agriculture has developed a lot in this area. The famous papyrus, a paper of vegetable origin used by the Egyptians, was also produced there.

HIEROGLYPHS

In Ancient Egypt, people did not write with letters. Hieroglyphics were used.

Hieroglyphic writing, or the hieroglyphic system, is what is called pictorial writing. Instead of drawing letters to form words, a "glyph" was drawn that represented either a thing or an action or a sound. This system is thought to date back to 3000 years ago.

Writing in hieroglyphs required a certain artistic skill. Only the privileged (pharaohs, priests, nobles) were able to write and read.

There are several legends about the invention of hieroglyphics, and most of them tell that it was Thoth who brought the knowledge and power of words to the people.

There were two very important events that helped us to translate the hieroglyphs:

In 1799, a French captain named Pierre Bouchard discovered the Rosetta Stone. On this stone was engraved the same text in two languages (Egyptian and Greek) and with three writing systems (hieroglyphic, demotic, Greek alphabet).

In the 1820s, Champollion, a renowned Egyptologist, compiled a complete list of Egyptian symbols with their Greek equivalents. He was the first to realize that the symbols could be syllabic.

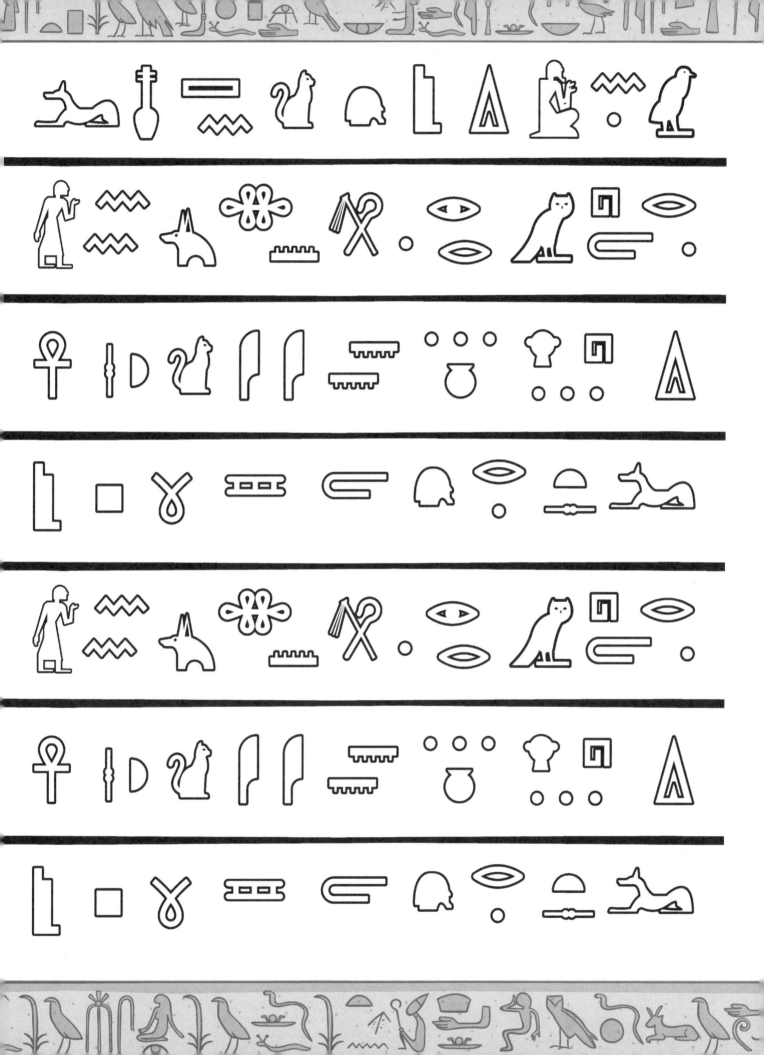

YOUR NAME IN HIEROGLYPHS

Using the table below, you can write your name in hieroglyphics.

For example, if your name is SCOTT, your name in hieroglyphics is written like this :

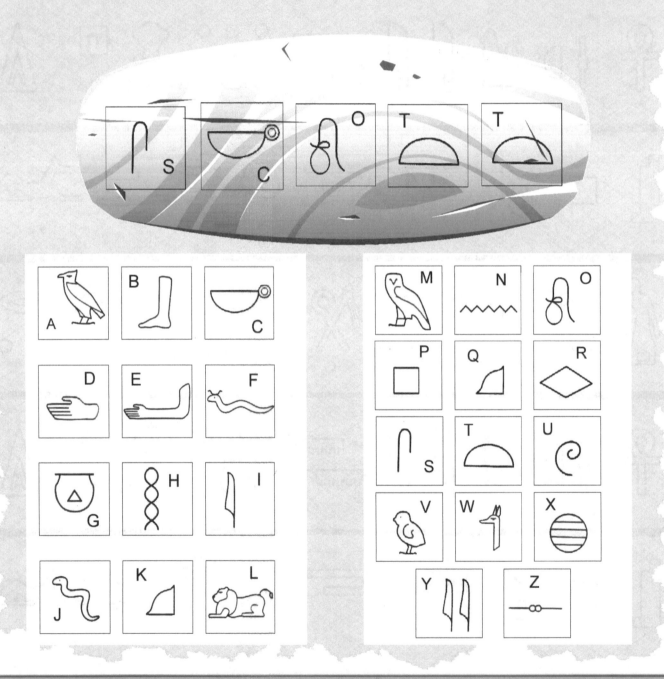

Write your name here

you can also write vertically (from top to bottom)

WRITING IN HIEROGLYPHS

Now you can even write a whole text, a poem, or a song with hieroglyphics.

MUMMIES AND PYRAMIDS

MUMMIES

According to the Egyptians, it was necessary to preserve the bodies of the deceased so that their souls could reach eternal life after death. This is why corpses were mummified.

The embalmers had a great knowledge. People who were mummified 4000 years ago still have skin, hair, and we can still see their tattoos or scars.

The word "mummy" comes from the Arabic "mummiya", which means "bitumen" or "coal".

It is thought that only the pharaohs were mummified, but this is not true. All Egyptians had this right, except for criminals. On the other hand, it is obvious that the mummification of a pharaoh was done with much more care than that of a farmer. Besides, there were several methods, some cheap for the people, and others for the important personalities.

Here is the method used for the pharaohs:

1.   The brain was removed through the nostrils.

2.   All the contents of the belly (organs) were removed except the heart (the deceased needed it in the judgment room, according to the belief). The inside of the body was washed with palm wine and spices. The organs were placed in four vessels, called canopic jars (or the four sons of Horus).

3.   The belly was filled with myrrh and sewn.

4.   The body was covered with natron* for 70 days.

5.   The body was washed and wrapped in linen.

The mummified body was placed in a coffin and then in a sarcophagus.

*Natron is a natural white mineral salt that absorbs water.

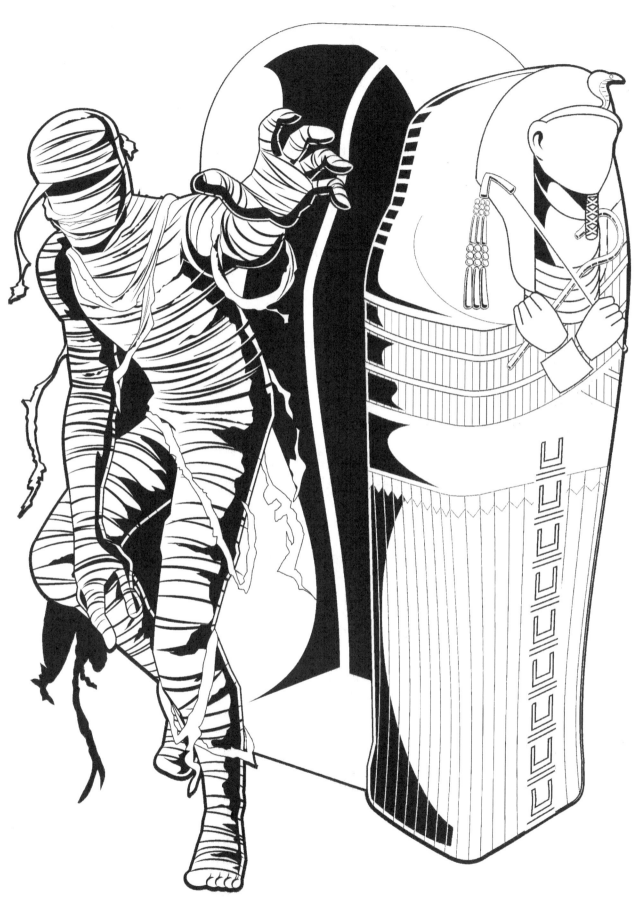

MUMMY - APPLE

To be made with the help of your parents

Material :

1 apple / 1 knife / 1 stick of popsicle / 1 cup baking soda / 1 cup of table salt / Large plastic zipper lock bag

SAFETY: Do not eat the apple or the mummification ingredients.

Step one:

Carve whatever you want into your apple (a face, or something else). Then attach the stick to the apple so it becomes a handle (like a candy apple).

Step two:

Mix the salt and baking soda in your plastic bag.

Step three:

Place the apple in the solution, making sure it is completely covered. Leave the apple in the bag.

Step Four:

Leave the bag upright and open so the moisture can escape.

Step Five:

Leave your apple in the bag for several days. Each day, check the condition of the apple. It will mummify as the days go by.

SARCOPHAGUS

A sarcophagus is a funerary receptacle (a box) designed to hold a coffin.

A sarcophagus can be made of stone or wood, and is most often placed above ground (not buried).

The sarcophagus is reserved for people of high rank. It is often carved with the effigy of the deceased, decorated and painted. It very often imitates the shape of a body (this is called a mummiform or anthropoid sarcophagus). For the pharaohs, the lid was decorated with precious materials (gold, silver, precious stones).

One of the most famous sarcophagus is of course that of Tutankhamen.

PYRAMIDS

To protect their sarcophagus and to put them in contact with the god Ra, some pharaohs had magnificent tombs built.

At the beginning, the tombs were rectangular buildings. They were called "mastabas". They were built on the west bank of the Nile, where the sun sets.

Inside, there was a room for offerings, and another room with statues of the deceased. Then there was a well that led to the burial chamber, where the sarcophagus was placed.

The oldest stone pyramid was built at Saqqara around 2800 BC, for the pharaoh Djoser (Or Djeser). It is the very known architect Imhotep who conceived it. It is composed of 6 mastabas, of increasingly reduced size and placed the ones on the others. This pyramid was 60 meters high. This type of pyramid is called a "step pyramid", and it looks like a big staircase (by which the pharaoh could go up to heaven and join Ra).

Later, the pyramids became triangular.

The most famous are the pyramids of Giza, dating from the 3rd millennium BC. They are each named after the pharaoh they house: Khufu or Kheops (146 meters), Khafre or Chephren (143 meters) and Menkaure or Mykerinus (66 meters). The burial chambers are in the middle of the building.

The pyramids were real labyrinths!

An Egyptologist entered through the top of the pyramid. Help him to find the exit. The solution is on the next page.

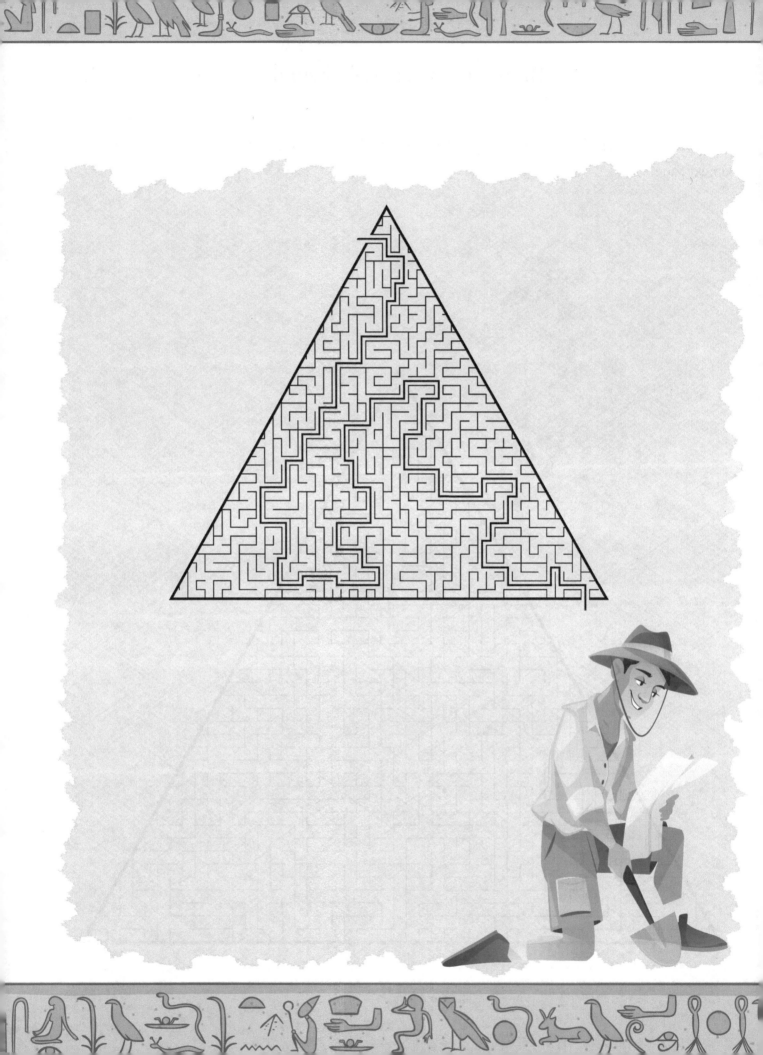

SPHINX

A sphinx is a mythical creature, with the body of a lion, wings of an eagle, and the head of a human or an animal (hawk, cat, sheep ...).

The largest sphinx is the famous Sphinx of Giza, located on the Giza plateau, next to the three great pyramids.

Egyptologists estimate its construction around 2600 BC. According to them, it would carry the face of the pharaoh Khafre.

There are other famous sphinxes: the one whose head is the portrait of the pharaoh Hatshepsut (now exhibited at the Metropolitan Museum of Art in New York), and the alabaster sphinx of Memphis.

The great Sphinx of Giza is one of the symbols of Egypt. It appears on stamps, coins, and is much visited by tourists.

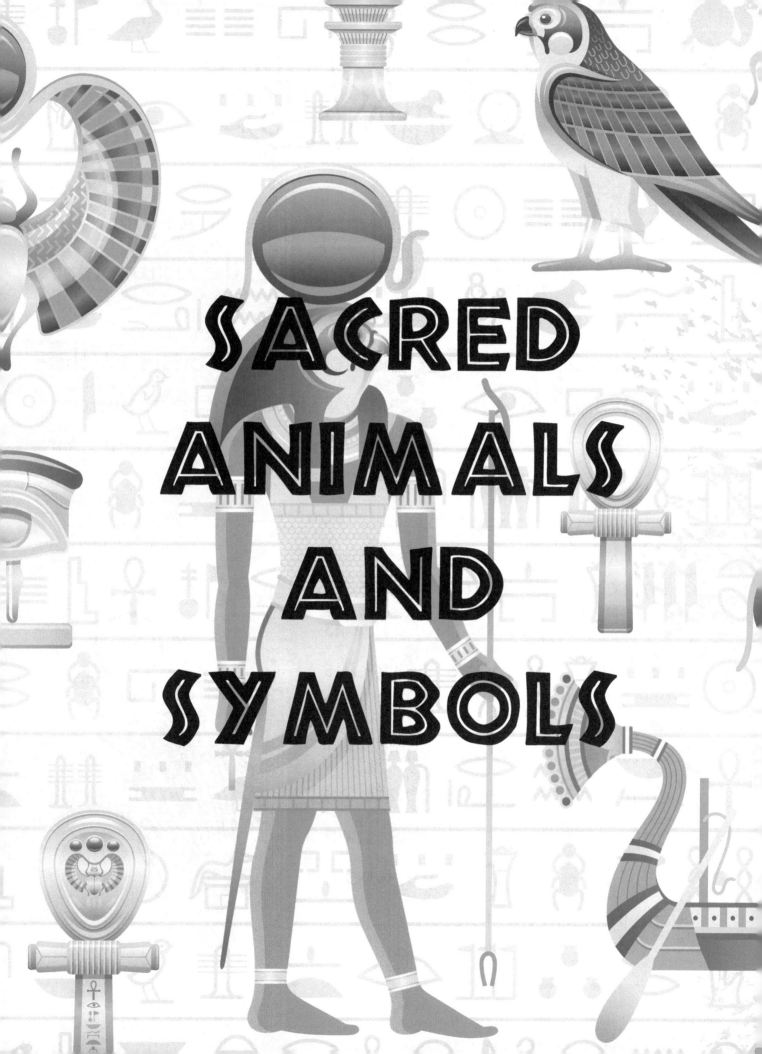

SACRED ANIMALS AND SYMBOLS

SCARABS

The scarab is a very present symbol in Ancient Egypt.

It represents the god Khepri, symbol of the rebirth of the sun.

The beetle called dung beetle is at the origin of this symbol: It rolls a ball of earth or excrement to its burrow. The Egyptians associated this behavior with the course of the sun.

There are many objects representing the scarab, such as jewelry, or the famous commemorative scarab, on which the pharaoh had a text engraved to commemorate an important event. It was then sent to each ruler with whom the pharaoh was in contact.

ANKH

The Ankh is a widely used symbol, and represents life and immortality.

It is also the symbol of the union between men and women, and especially the union between Osiris and Isis.

This union, according to the legends, caused the floods of the Nile (and thus also symbolized fertility).

The Ankh is also sometimes called the "key of the Nile".

The Ankh symbol was often drawn on the times, as it was thought to offer divine protection.

THE EYE OF HORUS

The symbol of the eye of Horus represents protection, healing, health and royal power.

It is also called Udjat.

This symbol, in the form of an object or jewelry, was widely used: It was worn as an amulet to heal, it was used in medicine to measure ingredients.

The legend tells that Horus and Set fought to replace Osiris after his death. Set would have torn out the left eye of Horus. Hathor (or Thoth according to the stories) healed the eye with magic.

It also symbolizes sacrifice.

THE FEATHER OF MAAT

The feather of Maat (or Ma'at) is one of the most used symbols in hieroglyphics.

The goddess Maat represents justice. It is said that the heart of the deceased was weighed with the feather of Maat. If the heart was lighter than the feather, it meant that the person was virtuous and could go to Aaru (the paradise ruled by Osiris). If not, the heart was devoured by Ammit (the soul-eating goddess) and the deceased was cursed to remain in the underworld.

The Pschent is the double crown composed of the Red Crown and the White Crown. This headdress represented the unity of Egypt and the control of the pharaoh.

The Red Crown is called Deshret, and symbolizes Lower Egypt (lands of the goddess Ouadjet as well as the lands of Set).

The White Crown is called Hedjet, and symbolizes Upper Egypt.

At the unification of Egypt, the crowns were merged.

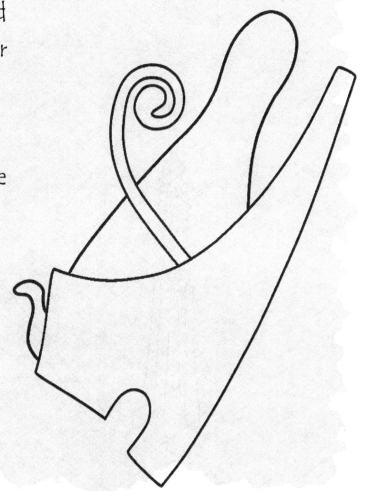

HEKHA & NEKHAKHA

Hekha, the Shepherd's Crook, symbolizes the power of the state over the people. The word Hekha was associated with Osiris and meant "to rule".

Nekhakha, the scourge, is the symbol of royal power, the control of the people by their pharaoh.

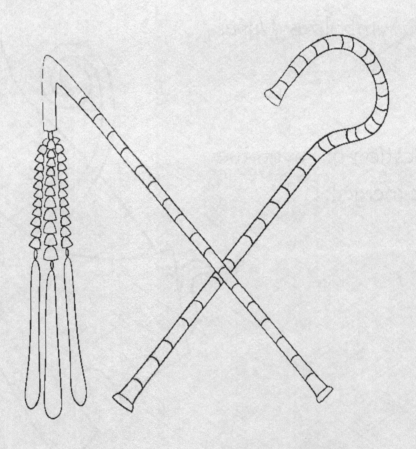

URAEUS

Uraeus is derived from the word "iaret" and means "the resurrected". This term is symbolized by a Cobra.

It represented the link between the gods and the pharaohs. Pharaohs often wore this symbol on their crowns.

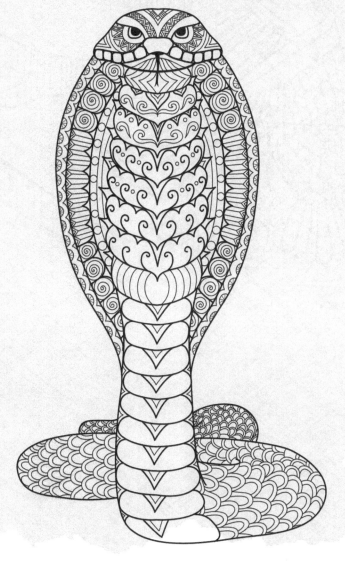

Uraeus is synonymous with the absolute power of the gods and pharaohs, and was thought to confer magical powers.

COLORING PAGES

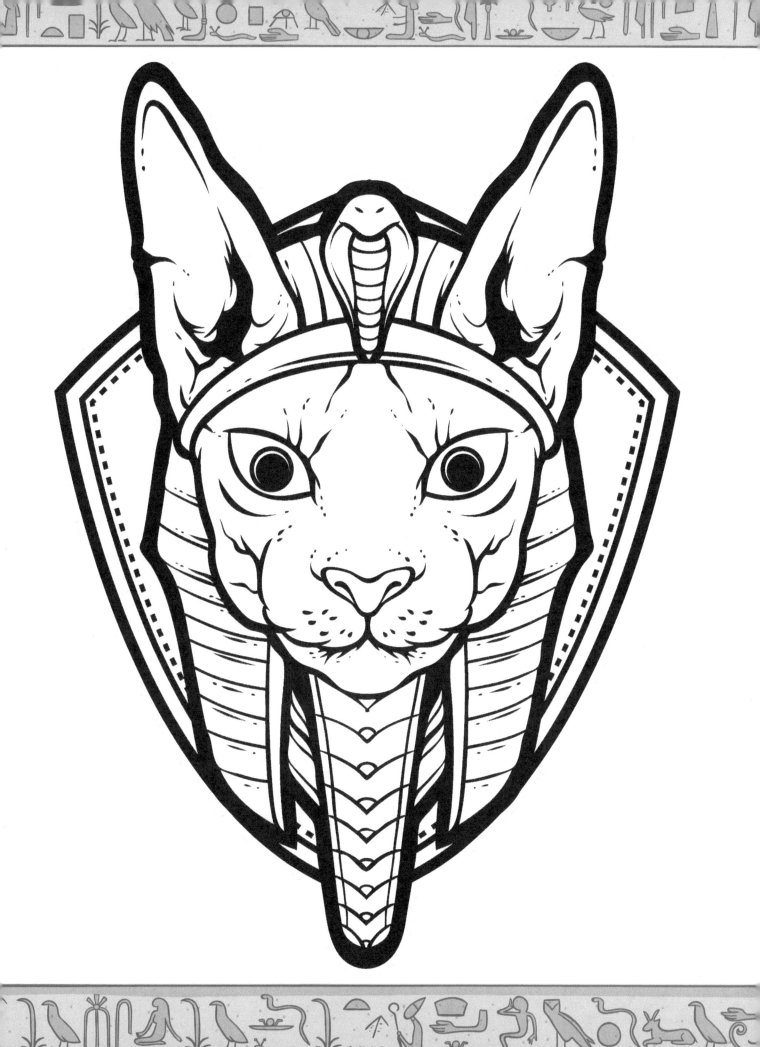

Made in United States
Troutdale, OR
12/08/2024

26093891R10053